BANSHEES PLAY WITH SHAPES!

BY THERESE M. SHEA

Gareth Stevens
PUBLISHING

Please visit our website, www.garethstevens.com. For a free color catalog of all our high-quality books, call toll free 1-800-542-2595 or fax 1-877-542-2596.

Cataloging-in-Publication Data

Names: Shea, Therese M.
Title: Banshees play with shapes! / Therese M. Shea.
Description: New York : Gareth Stevens Publishing, 2021. | Series: Monsters do math! | Includes glossary and index.
Identifiers: ISBN 9781538257357 (pbk.) | ISBN 9781538257371 (library bound) | ISBN 9781538257364 (6 pack)
Subjects: LCSH: Shapes--Juvenile literature. | Banshees--Juvenile literature.
Classification: LCC QA445.5 S54 2021 | DDC 516'.15--dc23

First Edition

Published in 2021 by
Gareth Stevens Publishing
111 East 14th Street, Suite 349
New York, NY 10003

Designer: Sarah Liddell
Editor: Char Light
Illustrator: Bobby Griffiths

Photo credits: p. 4 LaineN/Shutterstock.com; pp. 6, 20 Raggedstone/Shutterstock.com; p. 9 fractal-an/Shutterstock.com; p. 10 artshock/Shutterstock.com; p. 13 Claire McAdams/Shutterstock.com; p. 15 Rassamee Design/Shutterstock.com; p. 16 Yupa Watchanakit/Shutterstock.com; p. 18 Steve Allen/Shutterstock.com.

Printed in the United States of America

Some of the images in this book illustrate individuals who are models. The depictions do not imply actual situations or events.

CPSIA compliance information: Batch #CS20GS: For further information contact Gareth Stevens, New York, New York at 1-800-542-2595.

Find us on

CONTENTS

Words in the glossary appear in **bold** type the first time they are used in the text.

Have you ever heard of a banshee? A banshee is a spirit in Irish tales with a special purpose. They warn people that death is near. Scary! But what do banshees do when death isn't near? Perhaps, like you, they like to play—with shapes!

The banshees in this book love to learn about shapes. They might be able to teach you, and you can teach them too. Check your answers to the problems you'll read about in the answer key on page 22.

"BANSHEE" IS A WORD THAT MEANS
"WOMAN OF THE **FAIRIES**" IN THE IRISH LANGUAGE.

SHARING SHAPES

Do you hear the banshees **wailing**? It's a terrible sound. They're crying out so loudly because they can't remember the names of their shapes. Help them so they'll stop all this noise!

MONSTER FACTS!

IN THE IRISH LANGUAGE, BANSHEES ARE SOMETIMES CALLED *BEAN SIDHE*. IN THE SCOTS GAELIC LANGUAGE, THEY'RE CALLED *BAN SITH*.

BANSHEES ARE KNOWN FOR THEIR TERRIBLE WAILING, WHICH IS ALSO CALLED KEENING.

1.

2.

A. HEXAGON
B. PENTAGON

C. QUADRILATERAL
D. TRIANGLE

3.

4.

You can tell shapes apart by their features. One of these features is the number of sides they have. Triangles have 3 sides. Quadrilaterals have 4 sides. Pentagons have 5 sides. Hexagons have 6 sides. Use these facts to help you match each shape above with its name.

BOUNTING BORNERS

If you're out in the night and hear a banshee's wail, watch out. They're often carrying shapes to play games with. They love to **juggle** with triangles, for example. You could run into a triangle's sharp corners. Ouch!

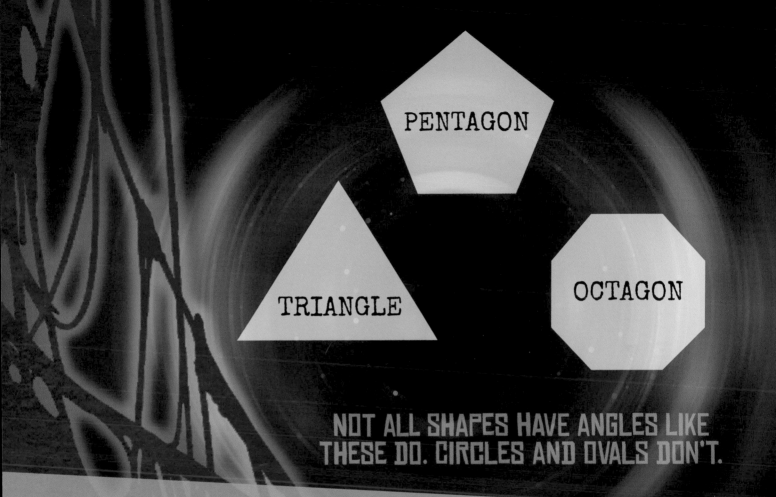

PENTAGON

TRIANGLE

OCTAGON

NOT ALL SHAPES HAVE ANGLES LIKE THESE DO. CIRCLES AND OVALS DON'T.

A shape's corners are also called its vertices or angles. You can **identify** shapes by the number of angles they have and the size of those angles. How many angles does each shape above have?

MONSTER FACTS!
A BANSHEE'S WAILING IS SAID TO BE SO HIGH AND LOUD THAT IT CAN BREAK GLASS!

QUA-WHAT?

Do you think the word "quadrilateral" is tricky? So do banshees! Just remember that the beginning part, "quadri-," means "four." Then, you'll remember it's the word for a shape with exatly four sides. Some quadrilaterals have special names!

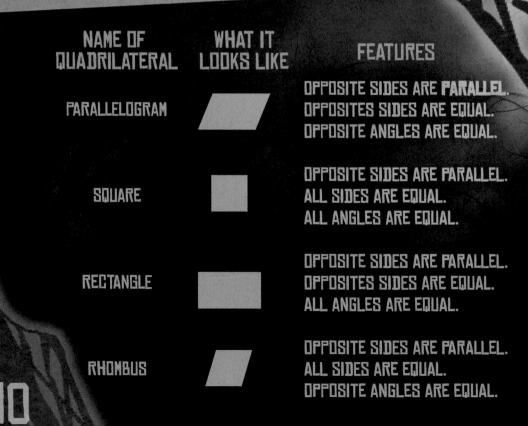

NAME OF QUADRILATERAL	WHAT IT LOOKS LIKE	FEATURES
PARALLELOGRAM		OPPOSITE SIDES ARE PARALLEL. OPPOSITES SIDES ARE EQUAL. OPPOSITE ANGLES ARE EQUAL.
SQUARE		OPPOSITE SIDES ARE PARALLEL. ALL SIDES ARE EQUAL. ALL ANGLES ARE EQUAL.
RECTANGLE		OPPOSITE SIDES ARE PARALLEL. OPPOSITES SIDES ARE EQUAL. ALL ANGLES ARE EQUAL.
RHOMBUS		OPPOSITE SIDES ARE PARALLEL. ALL SIDES ARE EQUAL. OPPOSITE ANGLES ARE EQUAL.

The banshees are playing another game. They're throwing quadrilaterals into a basket. But if they throw a shape that isn't a quadrilateral into the basket, they lose the game. Which shapes above should not be thrown in the basket?

11

2-D OR 3-D?

A banshee is trying to tell you something. First, it looks like a flat shape. Then, it looks like a solid shape. It's showing you the difference between a two-**dimensional** and a three-dimensional shape.

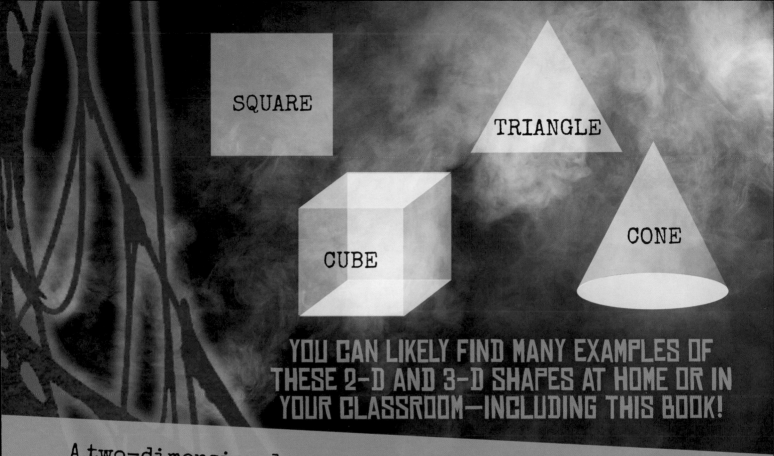

SQUARE

TRIANGLE

CONE

CUBE

YOU CAN LIKELY FIND MANY EXAMPLES OF THESE 2-D AND 3-D SHAPES AT HOME OR IN YOUR CLASSROOM—INCLUDING THIS BOOK!

A two-dimensional, or 2-D, shape has two dimensions, such as length and height. A three-dimensional, or 3-D, shape has three dimensions, such as length, height, and width. That makes it look like an object in real life.

MONSTER FACTS!
THE PEOPLE OF WALES TOLD STORIES OF A SPIRIT LIKE THE IRISH BANSHEE. IT WAS CALLED THE *GWRACH Y RHIBYN,* OR THE "WITCH OF RHIBYN."

FACE THE SHAPES

Banshees are often shown with long hair and a long **cloak.** Some tales say that a banshee can have one of three faces. It may look like a young girl, a woman, or a wrinkled old witch!

Did you know 3-D shapes have faces too? They're not as scary as a banshee's face, luckily! This kind of face looks like a flat surface on the shape. How many faces does the pyramid above have?

MONSTER FACTS!
BANSHEES HAVE BEEN TALKED ABOUT IN
STORIES SINCE AT LEAST 1380!

SOLVE THE RIDDLE!

Have you ever **solved** a riddle? It's a kind of word mystery. It gives you clues, but they're usually tricky. A banshee appears before you with a shape riddle. Can you answer it correctly? If you answer wrong, the banshee might put a **curse** on you!

SOME STORIES SAY THAT BANSHEES ONLY APPEARED TO CERTAIN ANCIENT IRISH FAMILIES.

FRACTIONS OF SHAPES

The spirits of the banshees in this book are trapped in their shapes. They'll play with them for all time, without rest—unless they can **divide** their shapes into equal parts! Look to the next page to see if they can divide their shapes and free their spirits.

MONSTER FACTS!

SOME PEOPLE THINK TALES OF THE BANSHEES MAY COME FROM PEOPLE SEEING BARN OWLS. THEY SCREAM AND HAVE SPOOKY WHITE FEATHERS!

Sometimes you can divide a shape into smaller forms of itself—or into other shapes. A shape divided into two equal parts is divided in "halves." A shape divided into three equal parts is in "thirds," and so on. How did each banshee divide their square?

You've had fun playing with the banshees and their shapes! Keep practicing identifying shapes and their features so you can be ready for more spirits that might be prowling—good or bad. There might be some in your math classroom!

The more you learn about shapes, the more you'll see them in your everyday life. From signs on the roads to blocks in a toy chest, it's fun to discover shapes all around. How many can you spot right now?

SHAPES MAY SEEM HIDDEN UNTIL YOU KNOW WHAT
TO LOOK FOR. SPOT THE SIDES, FACES, AND ANGLES!

21

GLOSSARY

cloak: a piece of clothing used as a coat that has no sleeves
curse: when magical words bring someone bad luck or trouble
dimension: a measurement in one direction, such as length
divide: to break up
fairy: a magical creature that looks like a very small human being with wings
identify: to find out the name or features of something
juggle: to keep several items in the air at the same time by throwing and catching them
parallel: describing lines that are the same distance apart at all points
solve: to find the answer
wail: to make a loud, long cry

ANSWER KEY

p. 7: 1. B.; 2. D.; 3. A.; 4. C.

p. 9: triangle–3; pentagon–5; octagon–8

p. 11: pentagon, hexagon

p. 15: 5 faces

p. 17: oval

p. 19: 1. fourths, 2. thirds, 3. fourths, 4. halves

FOR MORE INFORMATION

BOOKS

Brundle, Joanna. *Shapes*. New York, NY: KidHaven Publishing, 2018.

Nouvion, Judith. *Shapes*. New York, NY: Houghton Mifflin Harcourt, 2015.

Riggs, Kate. *Shapes All Around*. Mankato, MN: Creative Editions, 2018.

WEBSITES

Geometric Shapes
www.wyzant.com/resources/lessons/math/elementary_math/shapes
Read about more kinds of shapes.

Geometry
www.mathsisfun.com/geometry/index.html
Learn more about geometry and shapes.

PBS Shapes Games
www.pbskids.org/games/shapes/
Play some fun games on this website to learn more about the world of shapes!

INDEX